Sandra Markle

The Case of the
Vanishing Golden Frogs

A Scientific Mystery

M Millbrook Press . Minneapolis

With love for
Jeff and Jill Hay

Acknowledgments: The author would like to thank the following people for taking the time to share their expertise: Forrest Brem, University of Memphis, Memphis, Tennessee; Dr. Brian Gratwicke, Society for Conservation Biology, Washington, D.C.; Edgardo Griffith, El Valle Amphibian Conservation Center, Panama and Houston Zoo; Dr. Reid Harris, James Madison University, Harrisonburg, Virginia; Dr. Karen Lips, University of Maryland, College Park, Maryland; Dr. Joyce Longcore, University of Maine, Orono, Maine; Dr. Joe Mendelson, Zoo Atlanta, Atlanta, Georgia; Dr. Russell Poulter, University of Otago, New Zealand; Dr. Jamie Voyles, James Cook University, Australia; Dr. Kevin Zippel, Amphibian Ark, Apple Valley, Minnesota. A special thank-you to Skip Jeffery for his loving support during the creative process. A special thank you to Dr. Karen Lips for supplying the information for the map (on page 28) projecting the spread of Bd throughout Panama.

Main body text set in Johnston ITC Std. 14/21.
Typeface provided by International Typeface Corp.

Millbrook Press
A division of Lerner Publishing Group, Inc.
241 First Avenue North
Minneapolis, MN 55401 U.S.A.

Website address: www.lernerbooks.com

Library of Congress Cataloging-in-Publication Data

Markle, Sandra.
    The case of the vanishing golden frogs : a scientific mystery / by Sandra Markle.
        p.   cm.
    Includes bibliographical references and index.
    ISBN: 978-0-7613-5108-5 (lib. bdg. : alk. paper)
    1. Panamanian golden frog—Juvenile literature. 2. Frogs—Infections—Juvenile literature.
    3. Batrachochytrium dendrobatidis—Juvenile literature. I. Title.
    QL668.E22M37 2012
    597.8'7—dc22   2010042642

Manufactured in the United States of America
1 – DP – 7/31/11

Table of Contents

It's a Mystery 4

Frogs in Trouble! 6

What Is Killing the Frogs? 9

Frog Killer Found 18

The Race Is On 28

Search for a Cure 40

Will the Future Be Golden? . . 42

Author's Note 44
Frog or Toad? 44
Help Your Local Frogs 45
Global Rescue Efforts 45
Glossary 46
Digging Deeper 47
Index 48

It's a Mystery

High in the mountain forest close to El Valle de Antón, Panama, frog researcher Edgardo Griffith finds something exciting.

Edgardo Griffith holds a Panamanian golden frog. Full-grown frogs are just 1.5 inches (3.8 centimeters) long.

It's a Panamanian golden frog. In the mid-1990s, finding a golden frog in this forest would have been nothing unusual. In fact, the forest was so full of all kinds of frogs, it was noisy with frog voices. However, the world has changed—at least as far as being a safe place for frogs. Everywhere, different kinds of frogs are dying. They're becoming extinct, or gone forever.

It's sad to lose animals from the world, but the decreasing number of frogs causes another big problem. Frogs eat lots of insects. Some of these insects are pests that spread diseases and damage crops that people and animals need for food. And in Panama, the golden frog is treasured. Just as the bald eagle is the symbol of the United States, the golden frog is one of Panama's national symbols.

Golden frogs have always been important in Panama. In ancient times, people created golden statues of the frogs to bury with their dead. They believed the frogs would give their loved ones good luck in the afterlife. Modern Panamanians still keep statues of golden frogs in their homes for good luck. They don't want their national symbol to disappear forever.

These golden frog statues are being sold in an open-air market in El Valle de Antón, Panama.

Frogs in Trouble!

Scientists first realized that golden frogs were vanishing in 1996. That year biologist Karen Lips went to Panama. She visited the cool, misty, high mountain forest of Fortuna Forest Reserve in Chiriqui Province. She had been studying the frogs living there. When Lips visited that area for the first time, in 1992, the forest was full of many kinds of frogs. Each time Lips took a step, frogs hopped out of her way.

When she returned in 1996, the forest seemed

When Karen Lips first went to study Panamanian golden frogs in 1992, they were easy to find.

quiet. She heard few frog voices. Worse, when Lips started searching for frogs, most of the ones she found were dead. She collected the bodies, and soon had fifty of them. Finding so many dead frogs was surprising. In the damp forest, a dead frog quickly decomposes (rots and breaks down).

Or it's eaten by other animals, such as wasps. So finding lots of dead frogs meant that the frogs must have died very recently.

The deaths reminded Lips of what had happened a few years earlier just 60 miles (100 kilometers) to the west. There, in Las Tablas, Costa Rica, she'd discovered seven dead frogs. She hadn't thought much of that then. But when she returned to Las Tablas a year later, she found no frogs at all.

Caribbean Sea

Las Tablas

COSTA RICA

Fortuna Forest Reserve

P A N A M A

El Valle de Antón

Pacific Ocean

Miles
0   25   50   75

0   25   50   75   100
Kilometers

COLOMBIA

...ps are among ...many scavengers ...eat dead frogs.

7

Lips sent the dead frogs to a pathologist, someone who studies diseases and their causes. An exam of the frogs' skin under a microscope showed some strange-looking round sacs. The pathologist couldn't identify the sacs. But, he reported, they weren't anything known to kill frogs.

At that moment, Lips's career changed. Instead of studying the lives of different kinds of frogs, she focused on trying to figure out what could be killing them. One of the frogs she focused on was the Panamanian golden frog.

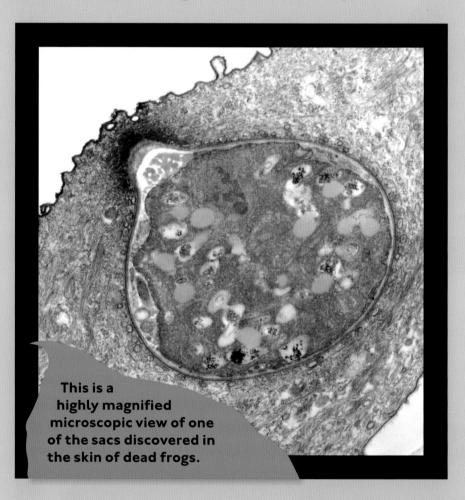

This is a highly magnified microscopic view of one of the sacs discovered in the skin of dead frogs.

What Is Killing the Frogs?

Could It Be a Change in Habitat?

Could the frogs be dying because a part of their habitat, the place where they live, had been damaged? Frogs, like all animals, need food, shelter, and a safe place to raise their young. A change to any of these things can lead to an animal becoming extinct. Golden frogs live in Panama's cool, misty rain forests.

Lips needed to figure out whether something in the frogs' habitat had changed. She'd seen rain forests being cleared in other places. The forest at Fortuna was untouched, though. It was too far from big cities for most people to visit. So the frogs' deaths couldn't be due to a change in their habitat.

Clearing this rain forest land for farming means it is no longer a good home for animals, including frogs.

What Do Golden Frogs Need?

Panama's golden frogs belong to a group of animals called amphibians. That name means "leading two lives." The adults and young, called tadpoles, live different lives. Adult golden frogs live on land. They breathe air through lungs and eat insects, such as ants, springtails, and termites. They need a habitat that has temperatures of 68° to 73°F (20° to 23°C). It needs to be shady and misty with high humidity. The frogs also need to be close to fast-flowing streams so they can lay their eggs in them.

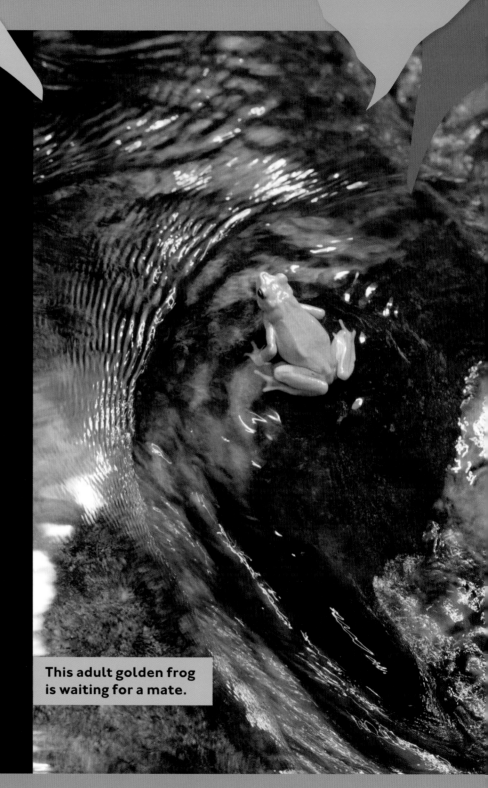

This adult golden frog is waiting for a mate.

The tadpoles hatch from eggs and live in water. The water must be clean and fast-flowing. It must also be just the right temperature, 69° to 72°F (20° to 22°C). Golden frog tadpoles breathe through gills, just as fish do. They have suction discs on the bottom of their heads. They use the discs to hold onto rocks. The tadpoles eat diatoms that live on the rocks. Diatoms are microscopic plantlike living things that lack roots, stems, and leaves. The tadpoles' mouths are lined with tough, bumpy plates to scrape the diatoms off the rocks.

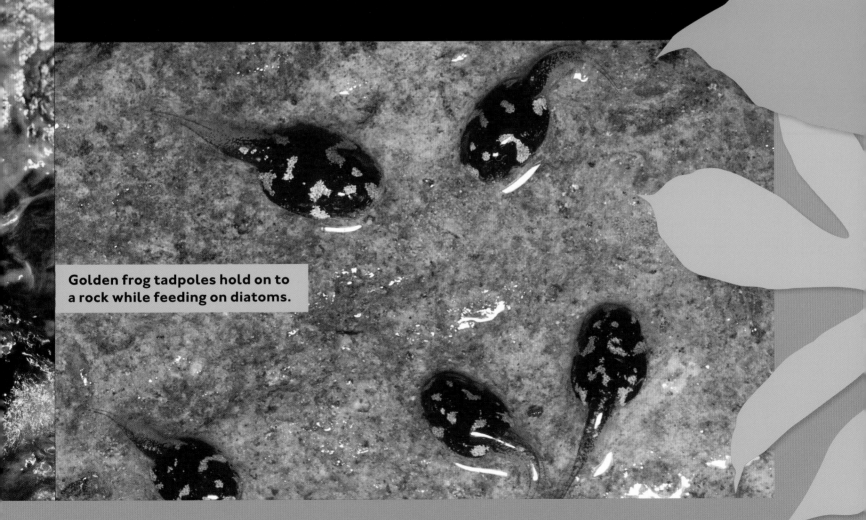

Golden frog tadpoles hold on to a rock while feeding on diatoms.

Could Pollution Be the Killer?

Lips wondered if pollution could be killing the frogs. Air or water pollution can hurt animals and even cause them to become extinct. But the forest at Fortuna was high in the mountains. Water only drained downhill from there. Polluted water flowing in from somewhere else couldn't be the problem. Fortuna was also far away from any factories. It wasn't likely that winds were carrying chemical pollutants into the forest. Pollution of the water or air wasn't the problem.

Chemicals and trash pollute a stream and can kill the animals living there.

Rain can carry chemicals from the air into streams, polluting the water.

Could Climate Change Be the Problem?

Climate is a region's average weather over a long time. Scientists have observed Earth's average temperatures rising in the last one hundred years. Rainfall patterns have changed as well. If the temperature of Panama's forest were getting warmer, it could become too warm for some kinds of frogs, like golden frogs. Or it could become too dry for the frogs to survive. Lips measured the temperature and humidity. Conditions in the forest were exactly the same as when the frogs were alive and healthy. She ruled out climate change as the problem.

Cool, moist forests offer a frog-friendly climate.

Most of the dead frogs Karen Lips found had patches of peeling skin.

What Else Could Be Killing the Frogs?

Next, Lips looked closely at the dead frogs she found. She wanted to see if their bodies had anything in common. Most of them had patches of peeling skin. All frogs shed and replace their skin from time to time, but this was more peeling than normal. Lips knew how important a frog's skin is to its health. She wondered what was making their skins peel. Maybe that was killing them. She sent a number of the dead frogs she collected to another pathologist. He took samples of each frog's skin. He looked at them through a microscope. Once again, the pathologist saw the strange sacs.

A Frog's Special Skin

All adult frogs depend on their skin to keep them healthy. Frogs' outer skin cells contain keratin, a tough, waterproofing chemical. It stops most organisms that could get into a frog's body and make it sick. It also keeps the right water balance inside the frog's body. A frog doesn't usually drink water through its mouth. It gets what it needs through its skin.

A frog's skin also helps it get all the oxygen it needs. An adult frog takes in most of the oxygen its body needs from its lungs. But especially when it is underwater, a frog also takes in some oxygen through its skin. This oxygen goes directly into its blood.

An adult golden frog's outer skin cells contain keratin, a natural waterproofing chemical.

Frog Killer Found

On September 16, 1997, the *New York Times* printed an article about Lips's discovery of the mysterious frog deaths. The story included a photo of a dead frog's skin that showed the strange sacs. Lips said, "I got a call from a scientist in Australia who saw the newspaper story. He said, 'Our frogs are dying and they have the same things in their skin.'"

Then a pathologist at the National Zoo in Washington, D.C., contacted Lips. Frogs at the zoo were also dying. And they had those same strange sacs in their skin. The pathologist wondered if they might be a fungus. A fungus is a kind of plantlike living thing that is unable to produce its own food and has to live off other living things. Samples of the skin and TEMs (greatly magnified microscopic views) of the sacs were sent to Joyce Longcore. She is one of the world's leading experts on aquatic fungi, or fungi that live in water.

Longcore said, "Luckily the TEM showed a mature zoospore, a reproductive cell with a whiplike tail. All I had to do was look at that, and I knew what the pathologist had found. It was a chytrid fungus."

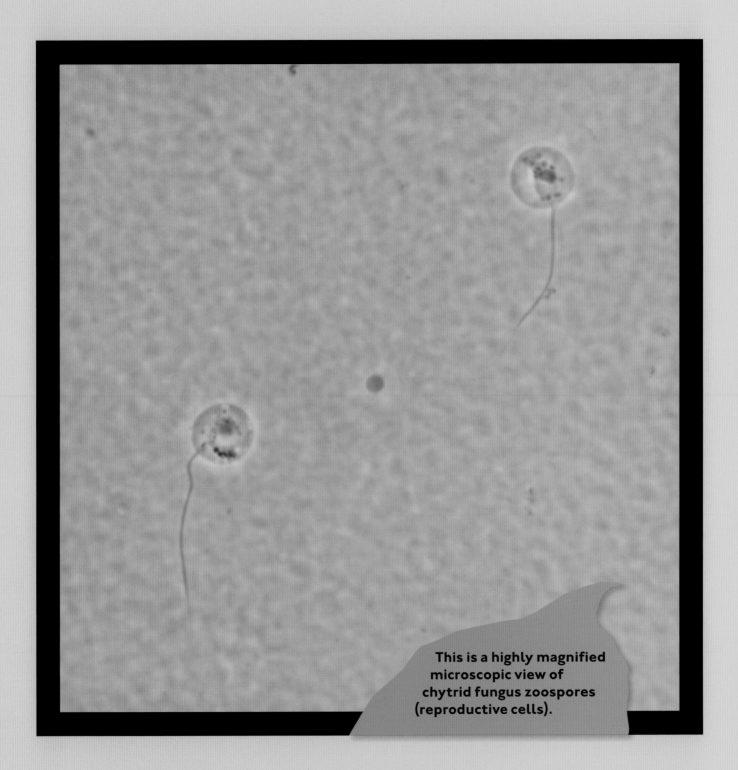

This is a highly magnified microscopic view of chytrid fungus zoospores (reproductive cells).

Chytrid is short for Chytridiomycota. It is the name of a whole group of microscopic fungi. They give off chemicals that break down tissue. Then they absorb the nutrients from the broken-down tissue.

Did discovering that a chytrid fungus was killing frogs solve the mystery? Not by a long shot. Until that moment, all the known kinds of chytrids in the world lived on protozoans (single-celled organisms), algae, plants, and invertebrates (animals without backbones). None were known to live on vertebrates (animals with backbones). This was a new kind of chytrid. Longcore and her research team gave the fungus its scientific name *Batrachochytrium dendrobatidis*. It's also known as *Bd*. Discovering *Bd* created two new mysteries.

- Could *Bd* be stopped from killing frogs?
- Could frogs survive long enough for that to happen?

This male golden frog is waving to attract a mate.

To find out how to stop *Bd*, Longcore knew she needed to understand how the fungus was killing the frogs. First, she learned that during its life cycle, the fungus goes through different stages. At one stage, the fungus is a cell, called a zoospore, that is able to swim through the water. This means that frogs can spread *Bd* just by sharing a stream or a pond. Once on a frog, *Bd* forms the saclike cyst scientists discovered on the dead frogs. The cyst produces rootlike parts that burrow down into the frog's skin. There the rootlike parts give off chemicals that break down the frog's skin tissue. The dissolved skin is taken in by the rootlike parts to supply food. Then the *Bd* fungus can continue its life cycle. But this damages the frog's skin, and the frog becomes sick.

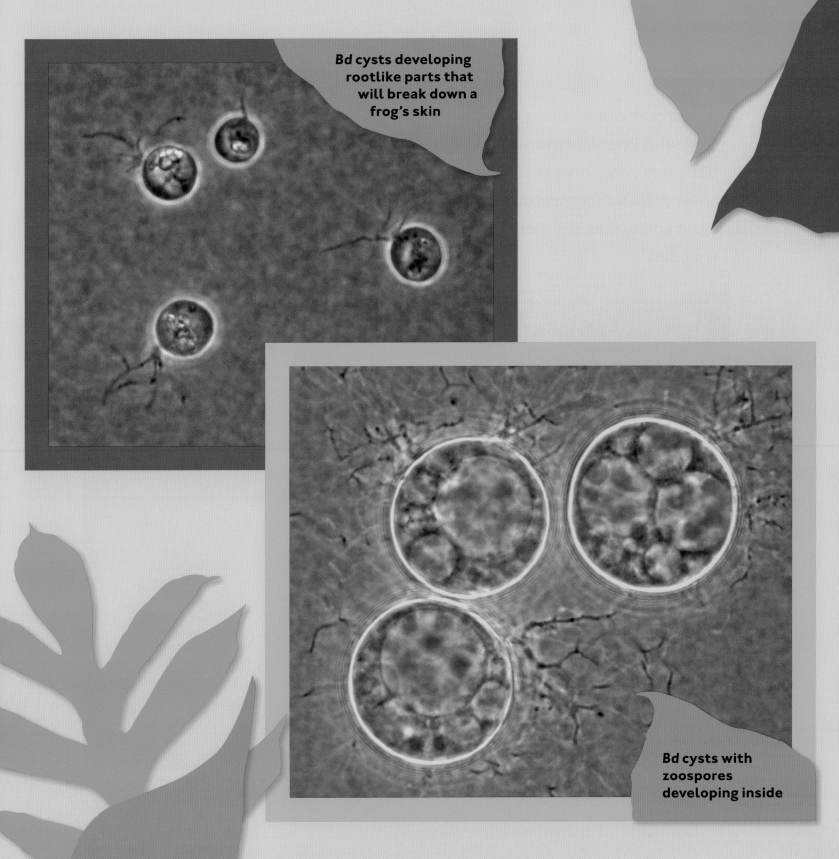

Bd cysts developing rootlike parts that will break down a frog's skin

Bd cysts with zoospores developing inside

Throughout its life, a frog regularly sheds some of its outer skin cells. A frog with *Bd* sheds more than just skin cells. Inside the *Bd* cysts, the fungus develops zoospores that enter the water. The zoospores in the water spread the *Bd* fungus to another frog. The life cycle of the fungus begins again and makes another frog sick. If enough of a frog's skin is damaged, the frog dies.

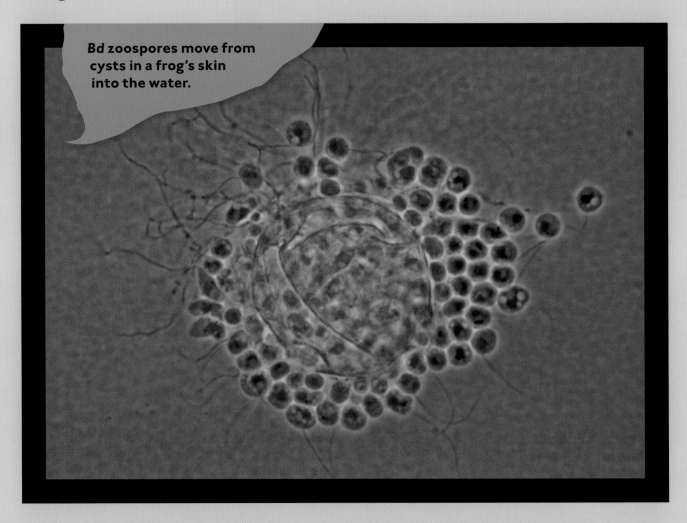

Bd zoospores move from cysts in a frog's skin into the water.

Scientists also discovered that *Bd* doesn't affect tadpoles. The zoospores only attach to cells containing keratin. All the surface skin cells of adult frogs contain this material. But only the cells lining a tadpole's jaws contain keratin. So even if tadpoles get *Bd*, very little of their body is affected. As soon as a tadpole becomes a froglet, or young adult, *Bd* spreads over its body. Then the frog becomes sick, and when a lot of its skin is damaged, it dies.

Changing from a tadpole into an adult put this young golden frog at risk of getting sick and dying from *Bd*.

Where Did *Bd* Come From?

Scientists think humans probably spread *Bd* to many places before anyone knew this fungus existed. Not every frog is killed by *Bd*. North American bullfrogs do fine even if they are infected. So *Bd* may have spread when bullfrogs were shipped from one place to another. North American bullfrogs are raised in ponds around the world to be sold for meat. People like to eat the frogs' legs. Some infected bullfrogs could have escaped, spreading *Bd* to local frogs.

North American bullfrog

The African clawed frog may have also spread *Bd*. These frogs can be infected with *Bd* without becoming sick. In the early 1930s, a scientist in South Africa discovered that African clawed frogs could be used to test if a woman was going to have a baby. To do a pregnancy test, a little of a woman's urine was injected into the frog. If she was pregnant, the chemicals in her urine caused a female clawed frog to lay eggs within twelve hours. A male frog produced sperm in the same amount of time. Large pregnancy testing centers kept as many as several thousand clawed frogs. New pregnancy tests that didn't require frogs were developed in the 1960s. After that, lots of clawed frogs were set free in local ponds.

African clawed frog

The Race Is On

In 1998 scientists from around the world gathered in Panama. They shared what they had found out about golden frogs and *Bd*. They knew *Bd* was spread through the water and by frog-to-frog contact. This meant it was only a matter of time before the fungus swept across Panama. Based on Lips's research, they also figured out that *Bd* could spread as much as 18 miles (30 km) per year. When this disease struck an area, scientists expected it could kill as many as 80 percent of all the frogs living there. Longcore told the other scientists that the best temperature for *Bd* growth is 73°F (23°C). The fungus does not grow if the temperature reaches 82°F (28°C) or warmer. That meant the Panamanian golden frogs, which live in the cool mountain forests, were especially at risk.

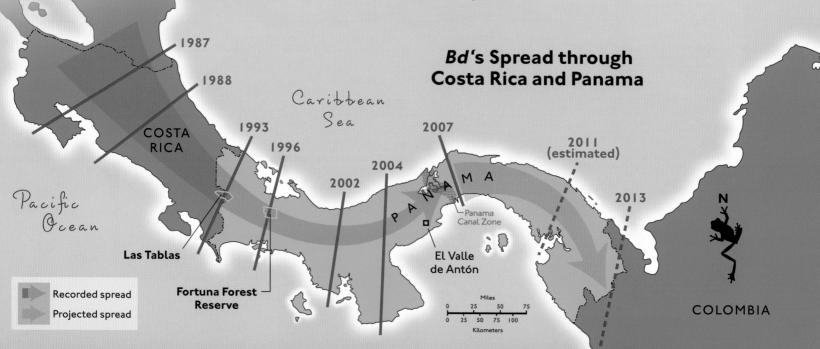

Bd's Spread through Costa Rica and Panama

1987
1988
1993
1996
2002
2004
2007
2011 (estimated)
2013

Caribbean Sea

COSTA RICA

Pacific Ocean

Las Tablas

Fortuna Forest Reserve

PANAMA

Panama Canal Zone

El Valle de Antón

COLOMBIA

Recorded spread
Projected spread

Miles
0 25 50 75
0 25 50 75 100
Kilometers

In 1999 Project Golden Frog was launched to help save the Panamanian golden frog from extinction. Its aim was to collect and breed golden frogs in zoos and other safe places. Kevin Zippel, cofounder of Project Golden Frog, said, "We needed to get out in front of *Bd*. We needed to collect golden frogs while there were still lots of them and they were healthy. But in the beginning, we didn't know what these frogs needed to survive in the wild. So we didn't know what we would need to re-create for golden frogs to live in captivity."

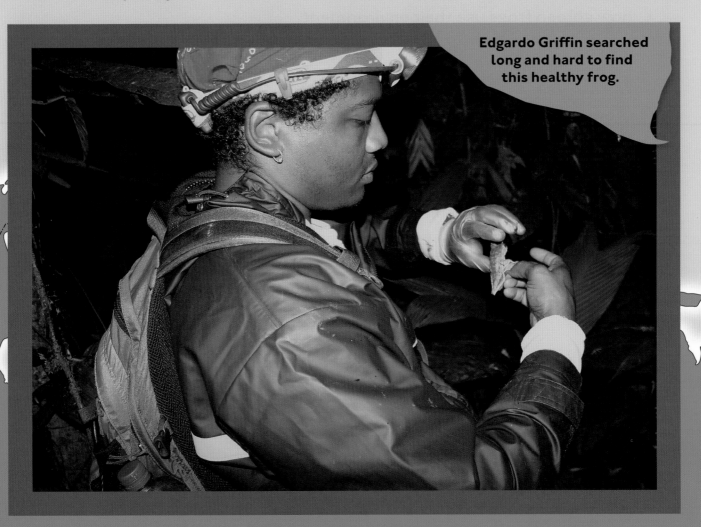

Edgardo Griffin searched long and hard to find this healthy frog.

Panama is an isthmus, a land bridge, between Costa Rica and Colombia. This meant that *Bd* could only travel into the country from the west or the east. Scientists already knew that it had come from Costa Rica to the west. They felt they had enough time to get out in front of *Bd* and collect golden frogs while they were still healthy. Then they could keep the frogs in special safe environments. But first, they needed to understand

- how golden frogs use their environment
- what conditions they need to survive
- how they behave daily
- how they behave during different seasons of the year

By 2000 the scientists working with Project Golden Frog had learned how to keep frogs alive and healthy in a safe environment. They were ready to start removing frogs from the forest to get them away from *Bd*. Those first rescued frogs were shipped to zoos in the United States and Canada. Populations of golden frogs are still living there, safely protected from exposure to *Bd*.

Zippel said, "We knew it was important for the people of Panama to have these frogs in their country. However, at the time, there wasn't any zoo in Panama able to set up and maintain the right conditions for golden frogs to survive."

The Houston Zoo partnered with other zoos to build a frog refuge in Panama. In 2005 construction started at El Nispero Zoo in El Valle de Antón. The El Valle Amphibian Conservation Center (EVACC) was created to provide a home for the golden frogs.

But while construction of EVACC was under way, disaster struck. Edgardo Griffith, who was studying the frogs at El Valle, discovered dead and dying frogs along a river there. *Bd* had arrived earlier than expected. The researchers needed to collect golden frogs quickly. But once they found them, where could they keep them?

Luckily, Lorenzo Hincapie was willing to help. He was the owner of the Hotel Campestre. Edgardo Griffith usually stayed there while studying frogs. Griffith was allowed to turn two rooms of the hotel into a temporary

The El Valle Amphibian Conservation Center (EVACC) was built to provide a safe home for golden frogs.

While EVACC was being built, the rescued frogs stayed at the Hotel Campestre.

Lots of frogs shared a room at the hotel, but each lived in its own plastic box.

frog refuge. He replaced the furniture with racks of 2.5-gallon (9.4-liter) critter keepers, special plastic boxes with lids that let air move through them. One of the two rooms was set up as a place to treat the frogs that might be sick. Then the healthy frogs were kept in the second room.

People from twenty U.S. zoos and other volunteers from around the world came to Panama to help rescue and care for the frogs. Every day the volunteers combed through the forest and streams, looking for golden frogs.

The volunteers also collected insects to feed the rescued frogs. And they tended the sick frogs during a ten-day treatment program.

Volunteers search streams and surrounding forests for golden frogs.

Because so many frogs worldwide had *Bd*, scientists had been working to find something to cure them all. They discovered they could use a fungi-killing chemical on the frogs. It is similar to one humans use to treat athlete's foot, a fungal skin infection. This treatment couldn't be used in the wild. It didn't work when weakened by a lot of water, such as in a stream or a pond. Also, in the wild, even if they were cured, frogs were likely to be exposed to *Bd* again and become infected again. The treatment worked well, though, for frogs in the special places built for their rescue. During the treatment, each frog was kept in a separate tank. The bottom of each tank was covered with a clean, moist paper towel that was often changed. Every day, volunteers gave each frog a ten-minute bath in a container of water containing a weak solution of the fungus-killing chemical.

A ten-minute daily bath in a weak fungus-killing chemical will ensure this golden frog isn't infected with *Bd*.

Meanwhile, the search for golden frogs went on. Both males and females were needed so they could mate and produce offspring. Finding male golden frogs was especially hard. The tiny frogs were easiest to find when they went to streams to mate. But once the males entered the streams, they quickly became infected. Males with *Bd* might also pass on the infection by wrestling with other males to defend their territories. Many male golden frogs died. But after a lot of searching, Edgardo Griffith and other researchers managed to find some in time. After these frogs were treated, they were able to mate with rescued female golden frogs.

Captive mating golden frogs offer hope for the future. A male (top) is only half as big as a female. Males were very hard to find.

Even though EVACC's construction was only partly finished, a special breeding tank was set up there. Some of the eggs the females laid failed to develop, but others were fine. The tiny tadpoles hatched and grew into froglets. After about three months, Project Golden Frog's goal of breeding golden frogs in Panama was a success. The cycle of golden frog life was continuing, even if only at EVACC and at zoos and aquariums.

Golden frog eggs

At EVACC, special tanks mimic the golden frogs' home habitat.

Researchers might yet find healthy Panamanian golden frogs somewhere. However, since 2008, only a few golden frogs have been found living in their forest home. The scientists remain hopeful, but golden frogs are clearly in danger of becoming extinct in the wild if they aren't already.

For now, only captive golden frogs remain safe from *Bd*.

Search for a Cure

Project Golden Frog and EVACC are buying time by keeping the frogs alive. Meanwhile, researchers around the world are trying to find a way to stop *Bd*.

Russell Poulter, a New Zealand scientist, and his team are among those searching for a way to clear *Bd* out of the environment. Poulter hopes to find a chemical that will kill chytrids but not harm the environment. Poulter said, "The goal is to have it work . . . not just on a flat field but in an . . . environment with rocks, bushes, and lots of different bits."

This potato field is being treated with a fungus-killing chemical.

Reid Harris, a scientist who studies amphibian skin, and his team are searching for a way for frogs to survive even when *Bd* is in the environment. Harris discovered that some kinds of amphibians, like the red-backed salamander, have helper bacteria on their skin. One kind of bacteria, called *Janthinobacterium*, kills any fungal spores that land on the amphibians' skin. Harris and his team are collecting and growing this bacterium. They bathe frogs in a solution of it. So far, this has protected the frogs from getting sick at least for a while.

Red-backed salamanders have bacteria on their skin that kill fungal spores.

Harris said, "The goal is to be able to introduce this helpful bacterium into the water and the soil in an environment. Then have it transfer to the frogs naturally and have frogs spread it to the water and soil in other places as they move around."

Will the Future Be Golden?

The high mountain forests of Panama are still beautiful, but they've changed. When the golden frogs vanished, their loss affected the lives of all the other animals who shared their habitat. Golden frog tadpoles were food for predators such as fish and young dragonflies. Their feeding habits kept rocks clean and kept algae from growing until it clogged streams. Few predators ate adult golden frogs. But adult golden frogs ate lots of insects. Their diet included mosquitoes, which spread diseases such as malaria and dengue fever. The people of Panama also miss this symbol of good fortune.

Colonies of golden frogs still exist in Panama, but all of these golden frogs live in aquariums. It's like being on board a spaceship, waiting to reach a safe planet. Will golden frogs ever be able to live free again? Researchers are working very hard to make that possible. For now, though, the idea of golden frogs returning to their home habitat in Panama is only a dream.

Author's Note

No tale of finding a serial killer could be more exciting than this true story. It was thrilling to track down and interview scientists around the world who worked on this case. One of my favorite moments was talking to Joyce Longcore and hearing the excitement in her voice as she told me about identifying what was killing the frogs. Then I became caught up in what other scientists shared about their race to rescue and preserve the last surviving golden frogs. But the story isn't over yet. The amphibian killer is still at large. Perhaps, one day, one of you will become the science detective who finally stops this killer. Then golden frogs and other kinds of amphibians living in protected colonies because of the threat of *Bd* will be able to return to their natural habitats.

European common frog

Golden frog

Frog or Toad?

Although they're called frogs, scientists group Panamanian golden frogs with toads. Golden frogs have smooth skin and long lean bodies like frogs. But like toads, they have special glands, called parotid glands, just behind their eyes. Like toads, when they are touched, golden frogs give off a poison through their skin.

European common toad

Help Your Local Frogs

The populations of many different kinds of frogs are decreasing worldwide. *Bd* is just one of the reasons this is happening. Frogs are also dying because of air and water pollution and habitat destruction. Here are things you can do to help your local frogs stay healthy:

- Encourage your family to think about what they spray, spill, and throw away. Never dump oil or chemicals on the ground. These substances could drain into local water sources and affect frog habitats.

- Work with an adult partner to keep local ponds and streams free of trash.

- Resist bringing frog eggs, tadpoles, or frogs home to watch or keep as pets.

- Always clean boots and shoes with a disinfectant, such as bleach, and rinse them well with water after wading or hiking around a pond or a stream.

- Ask your family to join you in reducing water use. This means less water has to be drawn from local resources. That will help preserve natural frog habitats.

Global Rescue Efforts

In addition to EVACC in El Valle de Antón, Panama, zoos and aquariums in the United States and Canada have Panamanian golden frogs on exhibit. If a zoo in your area is raising golden frogs, visit them. You can also check out these global projects to save frogs and other kinds of amphibians:

Amphibian Ark
http://www.amphibianark.org

Project Golden Frog
http://www.projectgoldenfrog.org

Glossary

amphibian: a cold-blooded animal with a backbone. Amphibians do not have hair, fur, or scales on their bodies. Frogs, toads, and salamanders are all amphibians.

***Batrachochytrium dendrobatidis* (buh-tra-koh-KY-tree-uhm den-droh-bah-TY-dihs):** the chytrid fungus that is killing frogs around the world; also known as *Bd*

Chytridiomycota (kih-TRIH-dee-oh-my-KOH-tuh): a group of microscopic fungi that live off other living and dead things by sending rootlike parts into them, secreting enzymes, and then absorbing broken-down nutrients. They reproduce through zoospores. They are also called chytrids (KY-trihdz).

climate: a region's average weather over a long period of time

extinct: no longer in existence

fungus (FUHN-gus): a plantlike living thing that cannot make its own food and has to live off other things

habitat: an environment where an animal lives and is able to find the main things it needs: food, shelter, and a place to raise its young

***Janthinobacterium* (jan-THIN-oh-bac-TEER-ee-uhm):** a kind of bacteria that kills fungal spores on amphibians' skin

keratin: a tough, waterproofing substance, similar to human fingernails

oxygen: a chemical in the air that is necessary for life

pathologist: someone who studies diseases and their causes

pollution: anything, such as chemicals or gases, that is introduced into and harms an environment

quarantine: enforced isolation

tadpole: the stage of a frog or toad between egg and adult

zoospore: a reproductive cell with a whiplike tail that is able to swim

Digging Deeper

To keep on investigating golden frogs, explore these books and websites.

Books

Aloian, Molly, and Bobbie Kalman. *Endangered Frogs.* New York: Crabtree Publishing Company, 2006. Explore just how sensitive frogs are to changes in their environment. Discover some frogs especially at risk.

Hamilton, Gary. *Frog Rescue: Changing the Future for Endangered Wildlife.* Westport, CT: Firefly Books, 2004. Beautiful color photographs provide a close-up look at endangered frogs and researchers trying to save them.

Markle. Sandra. *Slippery, Slimy Baby Frogs.* New York: Walker Books for Young Readers, 2006. Larger-than-life photos deliver a close-up look at the life cycle of frogs, including some that are truly unique.

Websites

Amphibians: Panamanian Golden Frog
http://www.sandiegozoo.org/animalbytes/tpanamanian_golden_frog.html
Discover facts about and see great close-up photos of the golden frog.

Green-and-Black Golden Frog Born at Bronx Zoo
http://blogs.nationalgeographic.com/blogs/news/chiefeditor/2009/03/panamanian-golden-frog-video-and-pictures.html
Discover more facts about golden frogs. Watch a video about Edgardo Griffith and his team working to save Panama's golden frogs.

Last Wave for Wild Golden Frog
http://news.bbc.co.uk/2/hi/7219803.stm
Play the video for a peek into the lives and behavior of golden frogs.

Index

amphibians, 10, 14

Batrachochytrium dendrobatidis (Bd), 20, 29–30, 35–36; life cycle of, 22; prevention of, 40; spread of, 24–28; treatment for, 35

chytrid fungus, 18–20, 22, 40. *See also Batrachochytrium dendrobatidis (Bd)*

climate, 14

El Nispéro Zoo, 32
El Valle Amphibian Conservation Center (EVACC), 32, 38, 40
El Valle de Antón, 4, 32

Fortuna Forest Reserve, 6, 12

Griffith, Edgardo, 4, 32–33, 36

Harris, Reid, 41

Houston Zoo, 32

keratin, 16, 25

Las Tablas (park), 7
Lips, Karen, 6–9, 12, 14–15, 18, 28
Longcore, Joyce, 18, 20, 22, 28

maps, 7, 28–29

Panamanian golden frogs: dead and dying, 7–8, 15, 22, 25, 32; eggs, 10–11; habitat of, 9, 42; protection and rescue of, 29–38, 40–41; skin of, 15–16, 22, 24–25; tadpoles, 10–11, 25, 38, 42
pollution, 1213
Poulter, Russell, 40
Project Golden Frog, 29–30, 38, 40

Zippel, Kevin, 29, 30

Photo Acknowledgments

The images in this book are used with the permission of: © Joel Sartore/National Geographic/Getty Images, pp. 1, 3, 4 (top), 6, 9 (top), 18, 28 (top), 40 (top), 42, 44 (top left), 47; © Brad Wilson, DVM, pp. 4 (bottom), 14–15, 31, 34–35; AP Photo/Arnulfo Franco, pp. 5, 15; © George Grall/National Geographic Image Collection, pp. 6–7; © Laura Westlund/Independent Picture Service, pp. 7 (top), 28–29; Edgardo Griffith, El Valle Amphibian Conservation Center (EVACC), pp. 7 (bottom), 38 (bottom), 39; © Dr. Elizabeth Davidson/Visuals Unlimited, Inc., p. 8; © Nick Garbutt/naturepl.com, p. 9 (bottom); © Bruce Dale/National Geographic/Getty Images, pp. 10–11; © Dennis, David M./Animals Animals, p. 11; © Ashley Cooper/NHPA/Photoshot, p. 12; © Gerry Ellis/Minden Pictures, pp. 12–13; © ZSSD/Minden Pictures, p. 17; Joyce E. Longcore, pp. 19, 23 (both), 24; Brian Gratwicke, Smithsonian Conservation Biology Institute, pp. 21, 33 (top), 35, 43; Zoological Society of San Diego, pp. 25, 37; © Forestier Yves/CORBIS, p. 26; © Tom McHugh/Photo Researchers, Inc., p. 27; © Dustin Smith, p. 29; Paul Crump, Houston Zoo, pp. 32, 33 (bottom); Mehgan Murphy, Smithsonian's National Zoo, p. 38 (top); © Nigel Cattlin/FLPA, p. 40 (bottom); © David Kuhn/Dwight Kuhn Photography, p. 41; © Michael & Patricia Fogden/CORBIS, p. 44 (center); © Stephen Dalton/naturepl.com, p. 44 (top right); © Geoff Dore/Minden Pictures, p. 44 (bottom right).

Cover photographs: © Joel Sartore/National Geographic/Getty Images.